50 Things
You Didn't Know About
Toilet Paper

By

J.S. Frank

A note on the photos

While researching this book, I came across centuries old cartoons and advertisements related to toilet paper that I felt like I couldn't not include in this book. Once I added them, I felt that many of the other pages needed a photo as well.

Therefore, I searched for and licensed several photographs and illustrations that are at least somewhat connected to each point. There were, unfortunately, a few points where I could not find a photograph that matched with the topic.

Also, the paperback version of this book does not have as many photographs as the eBook version does. It's cost-prohibitive my publisher to print photos in full-color and some of the original photos did not look right in black & white.

My profound gratitude goes out to each of the photographers and illustrators who have enabled me to do this.

Introduction

This book started out as a lark; an idea in my head at 3 o'clock in the morning.

Three million people search Amazon for the keyword "toilet paper" every month, I thought to myself. How many of them have ever given much thought to exactly what it is or the history behind it?

The three million searches every month, I should add, is a statistic that I came across while searching for something completely different. It was one of those details that once I read it, I forgot about whatever it was that I was originally searching for.

This led me to lying in bed in the pre-dawn hours one day, searching the internet for the history of toilet paper. This, in turn, led me to search for something else about toilet paper, which led to me jotting down a few notes about what I had read.

After a couple hundred Google searches and a few trips to different libraries in the following days, I had a list of 56 things about toilet paper that I had never heard about before. I wasn't far into this process when this seemed like an idea for a book. And so, I started writing.

I pared down my list of 56 things that I didn't know about toilet paper to an even 50 things. I did this simply because "50 things" seemed like a catchier way to start a title than "56 things about toilet paper."

I also want to add that I have done my best to pull these things from reputable sources. Moreover, I have included a bibliography with all of my sources for this project at the end of this book.

I hope you find these things as eye-opening as I did.

Number 1: Toilet paper began in China

The Chinese invented paper itself during the Han dynasty in the 2nd century CE. During this time, it was used purely for writing. No one began using it for any type of personal hygiene until approximately 400 years later.

It's not clear exactly at what point they began to use it to clean themselves. However, there is ample evidence that the wealthy in China were using it in that manner at least as recently as the 6th century CE. While some historians believe that they began to use it for personal hygiene prior to the 6th century, the evidence isn't clear as to exactly how much farther back it goes. (Needham)

By the early 14th century, according to Needham's research, it was recorded that in what is now Zhejiang province alone, ten million packages of toilet paper were manufactured annually. Each package is reported to have contained 1,000 to 10,000 sheets and they were often perfumed. (History of Toilet Paper)

Unfortunately for the rest of humanity, toilet paper would largely remain something that was used exclusively in China for another 400 years. For the time being, everyone else would continue to use wood shavings, hay, stones, or whatever else that could get their hands on to clean themselves.

Number 2: John Gayetty introduced it to the Western world

It wouldn't be until 1857 when a Westerner had the idea of using paper to clean up after one's necessities. That was when John Gayetty invented what he called "therapeutic paper". We, of course, now refer to his invention has toilet paper. (Mansfield University of Pennsylvania)

Joseph Gayetty was born Pennsylvania circa 1810. He later moved to New York City with his family.

Not much is known about his life prior to his invention in 1857. We don't know how he earned a living nor what it was that inspired his invention. Much of his life story seems to begin with him at the age of 47 when he made his now revolutionary invention. (Earley)

The only other details that we know is that his sheets of therapeutic paper were watermarked "J.C. Gayetty NY" and that he was incredibly bad at selling his invention. The only reason why we know about the watermark is because this fact is mentioned in one of the few surviving advertisements for it that is currently archived at the Library of Congress.

At this time, though, toilet paper was still sold in packages of individual sheets. It would still be several more years until manufacturers stated to put it on the cardboard tube that we know of today.

While Gayetty introduced toilet people to the Western world, it wasn't widely adopted. That would require more time, more improvements, and better marketing.

Personally, I'm still in shock that Mr. Gayetty decided to put his name on something that people were going to rub their butts with. The oddness of that one is astonishing.

Regardless, on the next page, one can see a public domain image of the only known surviving copy of an advertisement for these therapeutic papers.

Library of Congress, Rare Book and Special Collections Division, Printed Ephemera Collection.

Number 3: The Scott brothers get on a roll

Brothers E. Irvin and Clarence Scott of Philadelphia founded the Scott Paper Company in 1879. At first, they marketed their product from a horse-drawn wagon but with limited success.

In 1890, the Scott brothers decided to put their product on a roll making toilet paper look and perform like modern society is accustomed to seeing. Of course, there was a lot more to their success than putting it on a roll. The Scott brothers were also very innovative in their marketing.

Selling toilet paper was largely considered to be unmentionable at that time. In order to meet this challenge, the brothers offered local pharmacists a proprietary interest in their product by allowing them to design customized rolls. (Scott Paper Company)

While offering pharmacists an interest and allowing them to customize it might seem like a small details. It was an incredibly important change. This was what made them more willing to discuss the product with consumers. In turn, it helped them break into a larger market than they could ever get by peddling their product from a horse-drawn carriage.

Number 4: 83,048,116

83,048,116.

That's the best estimate that I could find as to how many rolls of toilet paper are used globally every day. 83,048,116 rolls of toilet paper every single day. (History of Toilet Paper)

That's a lot of toilet paper for the 7.7 billion who are alive today to use, especially since many people use a bidet or something other than toilet paper to clean themselves. (Worldometer)

Of course, as I discovered in the rest of my research, people use toilet paper for lots of other things besides cleaning ourselves. I will have more on that as we continue along on this journey.

Number 5: What is it made of?

Toilet paper is often made from virgin wood fibers, that is wood fibers that do not come from recycled paper or cardboard. When it is made at least in part from a combination of recycled paper, the pulp is mixed in water with chemicals to break it down as well as starches that give it strength while wet, and other chemicals to make it white.

Virgin fiber toilet paper is made using softwood and hardwood trees. Softwood trees include Southern pines and Douglas firs. These have long fibers that give the paper strength. Hardwood trees like maple and oak have shorter fibers that make the paper soft. Virgin fiber toilet paper is made with a combination of approximately 70% hardwood and 30% softwood. (Fischburg)

Of course, this is only how most of the mass market toilet papers are made and what they're made from. There are some specialty versions that are made completely different and are done using very different materials.

But I don't want to get too far ahead of ourselves.

Wood | Photo by Gregory Sinet on Unsplash

Number 6: Most expensive toilet paper

There is some controversy about this one.

The Hang Fung Gold Technology group is a Hong Kong-based company that produced a single roll of toilet paper back in 2016 that was made of solid gold. They did this to go along with the toilet they also made that year, which was similarly made from gold.

That single roll of toilet paper was valued at $2.5 million. (The Telegraph)

Of course, regardless of how much money one has, the fact remains that gold really isn't the ideal material for cleaning one's self. No metal is. That's why we use paper.

If we confine ourselves to only considering toilet paper that one might use as toilet paper rather than just to make a point then the most expensive option would come to us courtesy of the Hanebisho Company in Japan. (Spooky)

They make a brand of useable toilet paper that sells for $17 per roll as of this writing. While I have never tried this stuff myself, I'm told by online reviewers that it feels like wiping oneself with a cloud.

Who knows? Maybe if enough people buy this book, I might try it and include a review of it in the next edition.

Number 7: Toilet paper in space

Remember when I mentioned earlier that there's an estimated 4 billion people who don't use toilet paper because they use a bidet or something else?

There's one group of people who don't use either a bidet or toilet paper but are still worth talking that about. That would be the half dozen or so astronauts who are aboard the International Space Station at any given moment.

Wiping poses a risk of fecal matter coming loose and floating through the station. Therefore, they use a suction machine to dispose of bodily waste. (Molina)

And I think this is one of the things that keeps my life in perspective. No matter what other challenges that I must deal with, I have never once had to deal with the possibility of fecal matter floating around in my living quarters.

Astronauts earn every penny of their paychecks.

Astronaut on the toilet | Photo by Thomas Malyska on Pixabay

Number 8: Toilet paper is shrinking

You may not have noticed it but toilet paper has been getting smaller as the years have gone on.

The perforated sheets of toilet paper, which are the little squares that make up the roll, used to be 4.5 inches wide and another 4.5 inches long. Over the past several years, each of these squares have gotten either thinner, shorter, or both – depending on the individual manufacturer.

While this may not seem like much at first, when this is couple with the cardboard roll getting larger it can result in as much as a 26% reduction in the amount of toilet paper that a consumer gets with their purchase. (Lazarus)

It's not much of a secret as to why the manufacturers of toilet paper do such thing. They, like any company, always look for ways to maximize their profits. Make the individual sheets a tiny bit smaller allows them to cut their per unit costs and thus enable them to make more money from each sale. (Ng)

As an added bonus for these companies, most consumers never even noticed the difference in the size of our toilet paper rolls. I know I didn't notice it until I started researching for this project.

Number 9: Short versus long fibers

For those manufacture toilet paper, a lot of calculations go into getting the ideal mix of short fibers and long ones in the product. Longer fibers mean more durability, which many consumers like. However, short fibers are softer and will break down more readily in a septic tank. (Fischburg)

Thus, creates the need for an engineering and design trade-off when it comes to our toilet paper.

Do manufacturers use lots of short fibers, thus giving consumers the softness that they prefer as well as ensuring that their product won't clog a septic tank? If they go too far in that direction, they run the risk that it could fall apart while a consumer is in the process of using it.

And nobody wants that.

Do they instead ensure that no one will ever have a sheet of toilet paper that falls apart on them by using longer fibers of pulp? If they do, they must compromise on softness. Plus, it introduces the possibility that a consumer with a septic tank will have it clogged.

And nobody wants that either.

It really is an engineering balancing act to get the blend that makes consumer happy with all aspects of their finished product.

Also, in case anyone is wondering: no, when I graduated from college with my liberal arts degree, I never once thought that I would one day use the words "engineering" and "toilet paper" in the same sentence. Life is funny like that. This, of course, is one more way that this research project has changed me.

Number 10: Most popular brand

The most popular brand of toilet paper, according industry data, is the various private labels. This refers to those brands that manufactured by one company but sold under someone else's label. It's usually the "store brand" version of the product. (Shahbandeh)

Private label toilet paper accounted for $1.7 billion in sales during 2017, which is the most recent year where data is readily available.

When you consider that private labels are usually the cheapest of option in the store, the fact that they raked up $1.7 billion in sales in kind of impressive.

Among the name brand options, Angel Soft is the second most popular with Angel Soft bringing in $1.2 billion in annual sales. Charmin Ultra Strong and Charmin Ultra Soft came in third and fourth place with a little more than $1 billion each in sales.

And that is a whole lot of toilet paper.

I also thought it was kind of interesting that Charmin's Ultra Soft and Ultra Strong brands are so close to one another. It comes back to what I mentioned in my previous point about the balance between long fibers (the stronger option) versus short fivers (the softer option that isn't as likely to clog septic tanks).

I must admit that I lived most of my life without once thinking about what makes one kind of toilet paper stronger or softer. But now I know.

Number 11: Standards for the toilet paper holder

When toilet paper was first introduced, it wasn't on roll like it is today. Both the ancient Chinese and the 19th century Americans intended for it to be in a package in much the way that napkins or facial tissues are sold and stored. Manufacturers didn't begin putting it on a cardboard roll until well into the 20th century.

It's not clear how long it took for everyone to agree on standardized sizes. However, in modern usage, the cardboard roll is 10 centimeters long with a diameter of 4 centimeters. This works out to 3.9 inches and 1.57 inches respectively.

Oh, and I also learned that one can these cardboard tubes without any toilet paper on them. I was confused by this fact at first. However, I soon realized

There are also standards for where the toilet paper holder should go. The Americans with Disabilities Act mandates that in commercial buildings, it should be on the wall nearest to the toilet at a height of at least 19 inches from the floor. It should also be no more than 36 inches from the wall behind the toilet.

Not to be outdone, the National Kitchen and Bath Association recommends that the center of a toilet paper holder or dispenser be exactly 26 inches from the bathroom floor.

Again, I've never really put any thought into where the toilet paper holder Is located. Now, however, I have a desire to measure them every time I walk into a bathroom.

I need help.

Number 12: Largest Roll of Toilet Paper

Branson is small town in southern Missouri. It's a little more than 10 square miles in size and has a population of 10,520 people, according to the 2010 Census.

The town also bills itself as "the Live Entertainment Capital of the World" with Dolly Parton's Stampede and the Hollywood Wax Museum being just two of the towns draws.

Besides all of that, Branson is also home to the largest roll of toilet paper in the world. Charmin produced a roll that is 10 feet high and 9.73 feet in diameter or the equivalent of 95,000 normal sized rolls.

Needless to say, a roll of toilet paper like this wouldn't be stored in any location. This one is on permanent display at Ripley's Believe it Or Not.

If all the toilet paper were unrolled then it would cover more than one million square feet, which is an area greater than the base of the Great Pyramid of Giza.

The folks at Charmin estimate that it would take the average person 1,900 years to use a roll of this magnitude. But that does assume that you're willing to scale a 10-foot tall roll to tear off a piece of it when you need one.

Personally, I'll stick with my standard-sized roll.

Number 13: You can make it from sugar

For those who don't want to chop down trees to clean themselves, there is also the option of using toilet paper that is made from bagasse.

Bagasse is a fibrous by-product from manufacturing sugar. It's the pulp that is leftover once juice is extracted from sugar cane. It's also something would normally be thrown away.

However, there are several manufacturers who have started to use bagasse to make paper plates, carryout containers, notebooks, cups, napkins, and yes – toilet paper. Plus, the stuff is completely biodegradable and compostable. (QSR)

Oh, and since sugar cane is one of the widely cultivated crops on the planet with 1.8 billion metric tons of the stuff harvested every year, there is a lot of bagasse that is available.

A lot of bagasse.

By the way, bagasse from sugarcane processing isn't the only alternative to using wood pulp to make toilet paper.

A quick search of Google shows that there are at least seven different companies that make toilet paper using bamboo pulp. This is preferable from an environmental standpoint because, according to each of those companies, bamboo will grow back much faster than trees will.

Sugar | Photo by Conger Design on Pixabay

Number 14: Toilet paper cakes are a thing

I didn't believe it when I first heard about this but then I checked Google.

A quick search for "toilet paper cakes", however, found more than 309 million matches. Most of these matches, by the way, are recipe ideas and photographs of the finished product.

I didn't know that this was a thing until I started researching for this book. However, it seems like toilet paper cakes are popular at some birthday parties where the theme is a playful take on being "old as crap".

These cakes aren't really made using toilet paper. It is simply a cake that is made to look like a large roll of the stuff.

I just wish I could unsee what some folks have done with brown cupcakes that accompany these "old as crap" toilet paper cakes. I mean, seriously, people. Any joke can be taken one step too far.

There was even a moment while I was researching this book and I said to myself, toilet paper cakes have got to be the weirdest thing that I will find while researching this project. I mean, what could possibly be stranger than a cake that is made to look like a large roll of toilet paper that all your friends will eat?

I shouldn't have asked that question. I really shouldn't have.

Number 15: Toilet paper wedding dresses are also a thing

I'm not sure what surprised me the most: the fact that some women chose to make their wedding dress out of toilet paper? Or the fact that most of these dresses looked amazing?

But yeah, there are some women who make their wedding dress using several rolls of toilet paper.

When I discovered this fact, I had to stop my search for a moment. I needed a drink after learning this.

However – and I cannot stress this enough – some of those wedding dresses looked <u>amazing</u>. They were probably some of the best-looking dresses I have ever seen.

The folks at *Cheap Chic Weddings* started this as a contest back in 2004. The winning dress earns its designer $10,000 in cash with additional prizes of $5,000 and $2,500 for the second and third place entries. More than 1,500 people have entered this contest since it began.

According to their website, some designers have used as few as six rolls of toilet paper for their fashion masterpieces. Other designers, however, have used as many 74 rolls in their one of a kind creation.

The one question that I have not been able to find an answer to is: do any of these women actually walk down the aisle in these dresses?

Regardless, I would have loved to have a fly on the wall when they were brainstorming for this contest.

Number 16: Over versus under

It's one of the greatest debates in human history, in part because it's a debate that never really ends yet people still argue about. Should a roll of toilet paper be oriented to go over the roll or under it?

Science has stepped in to point out that the over technique reduces the chances of disease-causing bacteria being spread from the bathroom to the rest of the home or workplace. This is because one's hands make less contact with the roll in an over scenario and much of what dirty hands do touch goes down the toilet.

As a bonus, because of there being a lower probability of bacterial infections being transmitted, the over technique also results in lower employee absenteeism, higher workers compensation claims, and potentially even lawsuits. All of this is the result of that bacteria being transmitted from one person to another in the bathroom at their workplace. (James)

But will this bring an end to the over versus under debate?

No.

Of course, it won't.

This debate has been going on for as long as toilet paper has been on a roll.

In fact, and I what I'm about to propose is pure speculation on my part, it would not surprise me in the least if we one day discover evidence that the ancient Chinese – the original inventors of toilet paper – put it on a roll at first; only to switch to a package of loose sheets because of the over versus under debate.

Again, that last part is pure speculation from a guy who spent a few hundred hours researching toilet paper. Nothing more that speculation and nothing less.

But I would not be surprised in the least if some archeologist somewhere eventually found evidence to prove that such a thing once happened in ancient China.

Number 17: You can customize it

According to yet another Google search that I did while researching this project, there are a few hundred different companies that will customize a roll of toilet paper. I knew that there were people who did this as a gag gift.

However, I never realized how many options there were. You can even order your custom toilet paper in bulk from many manufacturers.

This is one of the simpler things that I learned and it makes me happy.

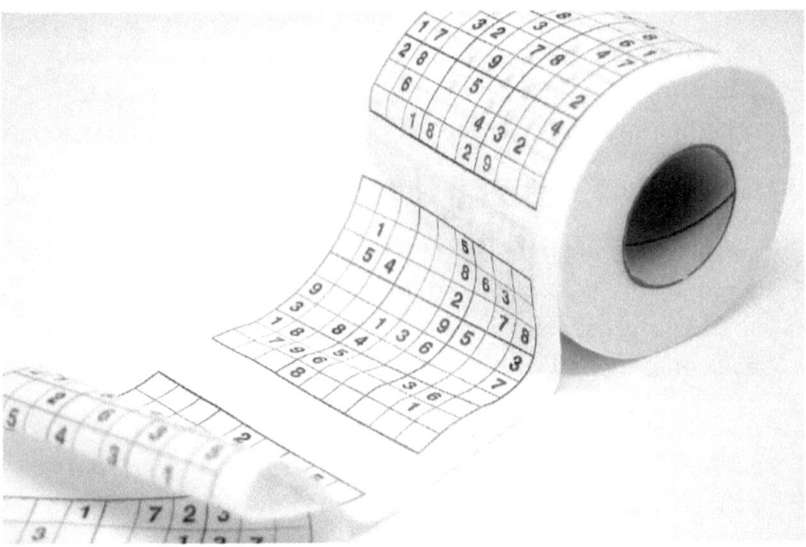

Image by Alexas Fotos on Pixabay

Number 18: Beyoncé only uses red toilet paper

In May of 2013, Beyoncé's tour rider was leaked online. A tour rider, by the way, is a document that spells out a celebrity's demands while on tour.

One of the more notable items on her list of demands is that she only uses red toilet paper. (Boone)

On a personal note, I must admit that before I did my research, I didn't even know that toilet paper came in colors other that white.

I suppose there is a reason as to why she insists on red toilet paper. However, in the half dozen or so articles that I read about her demands, no one ever seemed to ask that question.

Why would she want red toilet paper?

I suppose it could be a moment of pure diva-ness. There is also the possibility that, since red toilet paper is so different from the ordinary, seeing it allows her to know very quickly that she has been provided with a fresh roll.

This is again pure speculation on my part. However, after reading all of these articles, I'm going to guess and say that it's probably more a matter of wanting to know very quickly and easily that she has been provided with a fresh roll.

And if Beyoncé ever reads this, I would love to know her reasoning for it.

Number 19: Colored toilet paper

White is by far the most popular color of toilet paper, both in the United States and around the world. However, after reading about Beyoncé's preference for red toilet paper, I got curious about the other colors that it comes in.

The answer to that is: all of them. Toilet paper can be found in every color imaginable, if one is willing to put in the effort to find it.

This, in turn, led me to ask a second question. If white is the most common color, what is the second most common?

It turns out that the answer to that question is pink. Pink is the second most common color for toilet paper in the world. The third most popular color, by the way, is peach. (History of Toilet Paper)

Again, it's discovering these simple little things about our world that make me happy.

Number 20: Toilet paper isn't naturally white

Speaking of color, I suppose that I should mention that toilet paper isn't naturally white even though that's by far the most popular color for it. In fact, nothing that is made from wood pulp is naturally white – be it facial tissue, paper plates, or anything else.

Wood is naturally beige in color and it would normally continue to be beige when it is transformed into any type of pulp product, such as toilet paper. The change in color from beige to white is because of the manufacturers use bleaching agents to whiten it before it's packaged and shipped to stores.

I should mention that while researching this project, I found several sites online that warned about environmental and hazards associated with bleaching agents. A quick search of the internet found such articles on EnergyFirst.com, Prevention.com, TheIslander.net, and others.

I also found publications from the U.S. Forest Service and the U.S. Centers for Disease Control. Those publications indicated that, while there are some safety concerns with using it at the industrial level, there is little to no cause for concern at the consumer level. The difference is that these chemicals are used at exponentially larger amounts in the manufacturing process and that those risks simply do not translate to the individual level. (Hart and Rudie) and (National Institute for Occupational Safety & Health)

I also found a statement from the American Forest and Paper Association, which read in part:

Tissue and paper towel manufacturers meet consumer demand for bright, white products
using modern technologies that protect the environment and promote personal hygiene.

Concerns about toxins when it comes to chlorine bleaching in paper product manufacturing
are outdated fears relating to bleaching processes that have long been eliminated by U.S.
paper manufacturers. (American Forest and Paper Association)

With all of that said, after reading all these articles, I have found myself changing the toilet paper that I buy personally. I discovered that unbleached toilet paper does exist; it's beige instead of white but it does exist and that is what I have been buying since doing this research. For anyone who is wondering, there are some grocery stores that carry unbleached toilet paper and facial tissue. It's also available at specialty retailers and online.

I don't believe that there are any safety concerns about using bleached toilet paper. Whenever I use a public restroom, it's almost always bleached white toilet paper that's there and I don't give it a second thought. However, when I'm doing my own shopping and deciding what to buy, I can't help but find myself thinking that the bleaching process simply isn't worth it.

I feel just as clean after using unbleached toilet paper as I when I used the bleached white stuff. There just doesn't seem to be much of a point in bleaching it.

Anyway, that is simply my own opinion and a note about how this research has impacted the toilet paper that I chose to buy for my home. With that said, let's move on to the next thing that you probably didn't know about toilet paper.

Number 21: Celebrities use Amazon Fresh to buy theirs

Chrissy Teagan is a model and television personality who made her debut in the 2010 edition of the *Sports Illustrated* Swimsuit Edition. She's also married to singer/songwriter John Legend.

In response to a question on Twitter, Teagan indicated that most celebrities get their toilet paper by using Amazon Fresh. (The Dredge)

I guess this means that, in at least one regard, Hollywood celebrities are just like millions of other Americans. Many of us rely on Amazon to deliver our daily essentials.

Toilet paper | Photo by Alexas Fotos on Pixabay

Number 22: Toilet paper is a meme

After I found out about the world's largest roll of toilet paper, I started to wonder what the smallest roll of toilet paper in the world might be. It was researching this question that I stumbled upon the "Tear Rings" meme.

If you don't know what this is, congratulations. I envy you.

I would also recommend that you skip ahead to the next item on this list. The toilet paper meme is one of those things that, in my opinion, you are probably better not knowing about.

However, since Google found approximately 37 million references to toilet paper earrings when I searched for this, I feel that I must comment on it here.

This meme consists of tiny rolls of toilet paper that are (presumably) Photoshopped to look as if they were fastened onto a pair of hoop earrings. They are supposedly intended as a sarcastic response to people who are perceived as crying too much on the internet.

I'm not quite sure why the originator of this meme chose to go this way. Most importantly, I have no idea why he or she chose to use toilet paper as the object on these earrings instead of facial tissue.

Maybe I'm an absolute oddball. However, I do not generally reach for toilet paper when I need to wipe away tears. Toilet paper, in my opinion, is reserved for whipping something much different away.

When it comes to whipping tears, I have always used facial tissue instead. I don't know. Maybe I'm just odd in this regard?

On to the next item on this list.

Number 23: The smallest roll of toilet paper

Once I had moved on from the Tear Rings meme, I continued to search for information on what would truly be the world's smallest roll of toilet paper. After seeing the world's largest roll at Ripley's Believe It Or Not exhibit in Branson, Missouri, I halfway expected that someone somewhere else would have commissioned an exceptionally small roll of toilet paper and placed it on exhibit in a similar way.

Alas, I was not so lucky.

No one has done such a thing or, if they have, I couldn't find any record of it anywhere. I can only conclude from this that exceptionally small things do not attract a crowed the way that exceptionally large ones do. I feel that this is a bit of a shame.

Life needs balance. If there's going to be a tourist attraction that incorporates the world's largest roll of toilet paper, I feel that there should be a similar one for the smallest somewhere.

I know that this may seem like a weird thing to editorialize about. Regardless, this is one of the many thoughts that have gone running through my head while researching this project.

Now, to focus specifically on the question of who makes the smallest roll of toilet paper in the world, the only truly honest answer is, "I don't know."

I'm not sure exactly who holds this distinction. It would appear that no one has ever made a proper comparison of the various options to draw such a conclusion.

I can tell you, however, that the answer is almost certainly one of the travel-sized options for toilet paper. They are universally some of the smallest options one can find for toilet paper in the mass market. I'm just not sure which one of those travel-sized options hold the record for being the smallest.

Regardless, after seeing that this was an option, I immediately recognized the value in it. I can imagine many camping and backpacking trips where this would have been a much better option than any of the standard-sized rolls.

Knowing this not only gave me one small thing to look forward to on my next camping trip, it also restored a small portion of the faith in humanity that I lost upon learning of how popular the Tear Rings meme was at one point.

Number 24: Toilet paper thieves

In the United States or elsewhere in the Western world, it's possible that someone might steal a roll of toilet paper from a hotel or workplace. Not much that hotel managers or employers can do about it. It's often perceived as such a small cost of doing business that, unless it reaches ridiculous proportions, many in charge feel that it's not worth acting on.

China, however, has taken a different approach. The nation that invented toilet paper more than 2,000 years ago has now invented facial recognition software for toilet paper as a means to combat the theft of it.

The Temple of Heaven Park in Beijing is a popular destination for locals and tourists in the city's Dongsheng District. This 667-acre park was constructed in 1420 by Emperor Yongle of the Ming Dynasty. It holds some of the few sacrificial buildings that remain from ancient China. (Travel China Guide)

There are, of course, several public restrooms there to accommodate visitors. Unfortunately, the administrators at this park realized in 2017 that many individuals were stealing what they described as large amounts of toilet paper.

The Chinese government responded to this by installing toilet paper dispensers that incorporate facial recognition software. In order to receive any toilet paper, those visiting the restrooms are required to stare at a camera for three seconds. After that time, the machine will dispense a strip of toilet paper that is approximately two feet long. (Hernández)

No matter what one does after that the machine will not dispense any more toilet paper to that person for another nine minutes. This, of course, makes it much harder for visitors to steal any significant amount of toilet paper.

Number 25: The homestretch

Now that I am on number 25 on my list of 50 Things Your Probably Didn't Know About Toilet paper, I feel that I am in the homestretch. As such, I would like to take a momentary break from assorted facts about toilet paper to share a brief personal anecdote that is related to this project.

When I started this manuscript, I, of course, began with item number 1 on my list. From there, I went to item number 2.

My dear reader, I want you to know that when I typed "number 2" in a lengthy piece about toilet paper, well, let's just say that a plethora of sick jokes came rushing to my mind. I had to stop writing for a moment so I could recover.

I suppose the point that I'm trying to make here is that the act of writing this manuscript about toilet paper has changed the way that I think on many levels. I'm not sure if it's a change for the better or for the worse. I will leave that to you to decide as we continue through this toilet paper journey.

Number 26: 100 rolls per year?

Statistics about toilet paper and its usage are a little hard to keep straight. When I searched for them on the internet different sites and articles would cite one number or another for annual usage. The most commonly cited figured is that American household use 100 rolls of toilet paper per year. (History of Toilet Paper)

I've always been skeptical of any statistic that ends in a nice, even number. As a result, I decided to dig a little further.

The first thing that I noticed is that one of the same sites that claims that we use 100 rolls per year also claim that one roll lasts us for five days. There are 365 days in a year. If one takes that 365 and divides it by the five days it's supposed to take to go through a single roll, we learn that we should go through 73 rolls in a year; not 100.

Interestingly, most sites that talked about toilet paper usage do not cite any of their sources or methods. They will simply say that Americans use 100 rolls per household per year and move on.

Eventually, I found one site that used data from the U.S. Census Bureau and the Simmons National Consumer Survey to look at our usage. This study grouped Americans by how much they have used in the past 30 days.

- 41,450,000 people said that they used 16 or more rolls in the past 30 days;
- 135,760,000 said they used anywhere from 10 – 15 rolls;
- 94,370,000 claim to have used 5 – 9 rolls;
- 49,110,000 state that they used 1 – 4 rolls of toilet paper in the past 30 days; and

- 350,000 Americans say that they haven't used any toilet paper in the past 30 days. (Statista)

I presume that the last group is people who normally use a bidet. I mean, I really, really hope that they are using a bidet.

Number 27: Soft toilet paper may have helped control dysentery

Rates of dysentery dropped dramatically at the same time when soft toilet paper became more widely used in the late-1950s. There isn't enough hard evidence to conclude that there was a cause and effect relationship between soft toilet paper and drops in dysentery; only that they two things happened at the same time.

Even with the limited amount of data, researchers suspect that soft toilet paper was one of many things that collectively contributed to this drop. (Taylor)

To oversimplify things a bit, one of the ways that dysentery can spread from one person to another is when fecal matter isn't removed completely from a person's anus after a bowel movement. This allows for more bacterial growth and more bacterial growth means more opportunities for it to spread.

The working hypothesis put forward in the *British Medical Journal* is that softer toilet paper meant that people were more willing to spend enough time and effort cleaning themselves. This would have reduced the opportunities for bacterial growth and contributed to a decline in dysentery. (Taylor)

I know that this is only a hypothesis from one researcher. It is hardly conclusive proof that softer toilet paper had an impact in the decline of dysentery. However, when I think about his hypothesis, the entire idea seems so plausible that I feel I must mention it here.

I would love to see some more research done on what impact the introduction of toilet paper. I'm not sure how something like this could even be researched at this point since the decline in cases of dysentery began to drop more than half a century ago.

Still, I would love to see this issue explored in more detail by those with much more scientific and/or medical knowledge than I have.

Number 28: Toilet paper has prompted some weird laws

The United States of America is very much a hodgepodge of what at times seem like some really weird laws. Moreover, I hasten to point out that at least some of those weird laws apply to toilet paper.

For example, when one looks at the laws is Section 1563.23 of the Ohio Revised Code. This is the law that regulate underground mining operations in the Buckeye State. This law mandates at least one toilet for every ten miners and then goes to say:

> (H) An adequate supply of toilet paper shall be provided with each toilet.

I can't imagine anyone having a problem with ensuring that miners – or anyone else, for that matter – have an adequate supply of toilet paper at their workplace. However, the simple fact that this needed to be spelled out says a lot about working conditions in Ohio at the time this was enacted.

Of course, Americans do not have a monopoly on weird laws. In France, for example, Article L131-2 of the Monetary and Financial Code spells out that a check does not have to any special form or be on any special type of paper for banks to be required to honor it. This means, quite specifically, that you can hand a French bank teller a check written on a piece of toilet paper and the bank must honor it just like they would any other check.

While I wouldn't mind making a trip to Paris and may even use a bank while I'm there, I have absolutely no desire to see how their bank tellers react to checks drawn on sheets of toilet paper.

Number 29: $30 billion for toilet paper

The toilet paper industry is a global marketplace. In fact, according to news reports, this industry does a little more than $30 billion in annual sales, which makes for a lot of toilet paper. (Woodruff)

I know from personal experience that often times, people will hear a large number like $30 billion and not quite grasp the full significance of it.

Therefore, to help put that number in perspective, I would point that that if the toilet paper industry were a nation unto itself then, out of the 211 countries in the world, it would be the 100th largest economy on the planet.

The toilet paper industry essentially ties with Estonia in terms of the size of their economy and comes in as slightly larger than Uganda. (World Population Review)

I also want to add that this is only based on global sales of toilet paper. Almost every company that makes toilet paper also makes facial tissue as well as several other products. If we add all of those products into the calculation, they rank much higher.

Of course, I'm actually rather grateful that the toilet paper industry isn't a country unto itself. If it were then that would mean that the United States and the rest of the world would need to have diplomatic relations with it.

And I really don't want to think about the what the U.S. Embassy to Toilet Paper would look like. I mean, between the toilet paper dresses and the Tear Ring meme, this project is definitely starting to warp my brain.

Number 30: Spaniards love toilet paper

Once I started all of this research into toilet paper using the internet, I became curious as to what top level domains had the most pages that referenced toilet paper. I did a Google Advanced search that was focused on the keyword "toilet paper" and searched each of the 20 most frequented top level domains.

Top level domain, by the way, is the last two to four letters of a websites address. Examples of a top level domain include .com, .net, and so on.

It shouldn't be too much of a surprise that websites using the .com top level domain had the most references to toilet paper overall. There were 68.5 million pages ending in .com that contained a reference to toilet paper. This isn't all that surprising, though, since .com is by far the popular top level domain.

4.86 billion sites use the .com top level domain in comparison to only 1.95 billion that use .org, which is the second most popular top level domain. 68.5 million pages using .com and having a reference to toilet paper means that only 1.4% of the total .com websites.

This led me to wonder what top level domain the highest concentration of sites had a reference to toilet paper. First, I found a list of the 20 most popular top level domains. (Slawski) I then ran a series of 20 advanced searches on Google for references to that keyword on each of the top level domains. The results can be found in the table on the next page.

This research showed that, for the 20 most popular top level domains, an average of 2.63% of the pages referenced toilet paper in some fashion or another. In this light, 1.49% of all .com websites referencing it is surprising only in terms of how low it is. I presume that this is because there are so many things using .com that it gets drowned out.

The truly surprising result from my research is that .es, the top level domain for Spain, has way more pages referencing toilet paper than any other one. Of the 31 million websites that use Spain's top level domain, there were 4.96 million pages with a reference to toilet paper. This roughly translates into 16% of Spanish websites having some kind of a reference to toilet paper on it.

Canadians came in second with 5.96% of websites using the .ca top level domain having a reference to toilet paper. This is still well-above average but it's nowhere near Spaniard territory.

As for the top level domains with the fewest references to toilet paper, that distinction is shared by .edu, .gov, and .mil. Each one had a mere 0.01% of its webpages with the phrase toilet paper found on them.

The only thing that I conclude from all of this research is that, based on what I found for .es, Spaniard must really love their toilet paper.

Concentration of the keywords toilet paper, by top level domain

TLD	Source	Number of sites overall	Sites w/ toilet paper	Percentage
.es	Spain	31,000,000	4,960,000	16.00%
.ca	Canada	165,000,000	9,840,000	5.96%
.au	Australia	91,000,000	5,240,000	5.76%
.it	Italy	55,200,000	2,740,000	4.96%
.ch	Switzerland	62,100,000	2,740,000	4.41%
.fr	France	96,700,000	3,140,000	3.25%
.ru	Russian Federation	67,900,000	2,060,000	3.03%
.de	Germany	145,000,000	3,460,000	2.39%
.uk	United Kingdom	473,000,000	9,700,000	2.05%
.no	Norway	32,300,000	470,000	1.46%
.com	Commercial	4,860,000,000	68,500,000	1.41%
.net	Network services	206,000,000	1,330,000	0.65%
.se	Sweden	39,000,000	199,000	0.51%
.nl	Netherlands	45,700,000	170,000	0.37%
.jp	Japan	139,000,000	267,000	0.19%
.us	United States	68,300,000	83,400	0.12%
.org	Noncommercial	1,950,000,000	1,420,000	0.07%
.mil	U.S. Military	28,400,000	2,770	0.01%

.gov	U.S. Government	1,060,000,000	72,400	0.01%
.edu	Educational institutions	1,550,000,000	85,500	0.01%
			Average	**2.63%**

Data from Google Advanced Searches. November 1, 2019

Number 31: Brits could face a shortage

The United Kingdom held a referendum on June 23, 2017. Voters were asked one question: should their nation remain in the European Union?

It was a controversial referendum. Wild claims and counterclaims were made by the supporters of both options. Prime Minister Tony Blair staked his career on the majority of voters choosing to remain in the European Union.

However, when the dust finally settled, 51.9% of Britons voted to leave the European Union. Blair resigned from office the next day and the British public began to ask questions about what this would mean. (Khetani-Shah and Deutsch)

One of the more repeated claims is that the British will face a shortage of toilet paper because of Brexit. This is because their toilet paper is entirely imported from continental Europe, which wasn't a problem while they were still in the European Union. However, with the prospect of them leaving, all of that is jeopardy.

There will likely be delays at the border and in ports of entry. Those delays would likely cause a shortage of the staples that are being imported, which includes toilet paper.

In my research for this project, I found 18 published articles that predicted a coming shortage of the stuff while only one said that there wouldn't be any shortages at all. Only time will tell which side is correct with any degree of accuracy.

Regardless, if I were living in London right now, I'd definitely be stocking up.

Number 32: Johnny Carson caused a shortage of it

There are anecdotes in the television business and then there are legends. The Great Toilet Paper Scare of 1973? That was the stuff of legend.

It started simply enough. Johnny Carson, then host of *The Tonight Show* on NBC, began his nightly monologue much like he did every other night during his career the evening of December 19, 1973. During his broadcast, he said one joke that changed everything.

> You know, we've got all sorts of shortages these days. But have you heard the latest? I'm not kidding. I saw it in the papers. There's an acute shortage of…of toilet paper!

33 words that were said before a televised audience of 20 million Americans was all that it took to launch a panic. Carson intended this a joke but people still rushed to stores buying all of the toilet paper they could get their hands on.

The result was a nationwide shortage of toilet paper. Carson apologized for the damage that his joke had done but store shelves were still empty of toilet paper. (Shaerf)

Number 33: National Toilet Paper Day

Thanks to the internet, there is pretty much a holiday for everything. Toilet paper is no exception. August 26 is National Toilet Paper Day.

During my research, I tried to discover when this observance started as well as whose idea it was. Alas, I was not able to find a definitive answer to either of those questions.

The best that I was able to discern comes from an article written by Gloria Feldt that was published on August 24, 2007 in *Women's Voice for Change*. Her article is entitled "August 26: National Women's Equality – Oops – Toilet Paper Day."

Her piece laments the fact that she wasn't able to find a greeting card for National Women's Equity Day – a day to celebrate women getting the vote in the United States – but found several on National Toilet Paper Day. Oh, and both National Women's Equity Day and National Toilet Paper Day are both on August 26.

I'll refrain from making any comments about a holiday dedicated to toilet paper getting more recognition than the anniversary of half the population being able to vote. There's simply nothing I can add to what she wrote.

Regardless, my point here is that her article establishes that National Toilet Paper Day was happening as far back as 2007. How much farther back, though, is still a bit of a mystery.

An even bigger mystery is who had the idea to celebrate it on August 26 and why.

Number 34: It's all about the ply

From the category of "I Can't Believe I Didn't Realize That" is a factoid about plies of toilet paper.

But first, some context.

The plies in toilet paper refer to individual layers of individual sheets that are fused together. Thus, one-ply toilet paper is a single sheet, two-ply is two sheets fused together, three-ply is three sheets fused together, and so on. Adding the extra plies gives the final product more durability and is often cheaper than manufacturing one single non-plied sheet with the thickness of a plied option. (Clean It Supply)

I basically knew all of that before starting this research project. What I didn't realize that the ply technique that gives us two- or three-ply toilet paper is also the basis for plywood.

I don't know why I didn't realize that earlier. It's obvious if you think about it for half a second but I get never really thought about either toilet paper or plywood enough to make the connection.

Three rolls of toilet paper – Photo by Michael Jasmund on Unsplash

Number 35: TP parties

There was a moment earlier on in my research when I thought that I would have to at least mention toilet parties. They're obnoxious and immature. They involve a group of (almost always) teenagers covering someone house and yard with rolls and rolls of toilet paper.

I thought I would have to include that, but then I noticed something odd while researching this. I could find very references to TP parties (as in toilet paper parties) online. However, I found lots and lots about TP parties (as in tee-pee parties).

These are party set up in or around a tee-pee. Again, this is simply not something that I was expecting.

Back to shortages of toilet paper more a moment, but this time in Venezuela.

The government of Venezuela instituted a series of price controls. These measures set fixed prices for a multitude of consumer products, which included toilet paper. They also made it illegal for anyone to sell a product at a price different from the one they arbitrarily set.

The Venezuelan governments also decreed an official exchange rate for their currency. One U.S. dollar, in their state-controlled exchange system, would be worth 6.35 Venezuelan bolivars.

Problems began to arise when people realized that there was a massive difference between what the government-sanctioned values were inside Venezuela and what everything was worth in the free-market outside of their country. I became possible for people to buy toilet paper at the official price in Venezuela and sell it overseas with a huge profit margin. (Bird)

Selling toilet paper overseas was, of course, illegal. However, the amount of money that people could make doing it was so large that there were always individuals willing to do so.

Buying toilet paper at the official price in Venezuela and selling if for huge profits overseas was great for those individuals who did it without getting caught. Catastrophe arose, however, is that this also meant that there was little to no toilet paper left for regular people to use. It was all being sold overseas for a profit.

And that is how price controls caused a shortage of toilet paper in Venezuela.

Number 37: Military usages

I came across several anecdotes about toilet paper. Many were nothing more than rumors Some turned out to be true. Others are just head-scratchers.

One of the ones that left me uncertain as to whether or not to believe it is the claim the U.S. Army used toilet paper to camouflage its tanks in Saudi Arabia during Operation: Desert Storm. (Wolf)

These claims weren't just on social media or internet bulletin boards. There were legitimate mainstream news organizations who reported this. I couldn't find anything from the U.S. Army about this nor could I find anything about what techniques they used to camouflage tanks back in 1991.

The idea seems too strange to be true, but then again so do toilet paper cakes and toilet paper wedding dresses. In fact, this one seems so strange that it might actually be true.

Number 38: Hate is for assholes

The German non-profit Goldeimer took to pulping Nazi election pamphlets back in 2017. They then turned that paper pulp into toilet paper. They called this campaign "hate is for assholes."

A representative of the group was quoted as saying, "In Germany, hatred has once again taken hold of the political climate. This is somewhat unfortunate. That is why Goldeimer is calling for a hate-free campaign. Up until the federal election, all campaign material that incites hatred and causes hurt will be taken out of circulation. Afterwards, from the crude slogans, we will make a velvety-soft special edition toilet paper."

All money raised was donated to the CURA organization, which aids victims of right-wing violence. The toilet paper sold out in less than 24 hours. (DW)

Number 39: Toilegami

Toilegami is origami, the Japanese art of paper folding, that is done with toilet paper. A skilled artist can do almost anything with toilet paper that they otherwise could do with any other type of paper, although I'm told that it's easier with the thicker, heavier grades of toilet paper.

Unfortunately, I was not able to obtain a license to show any of the resulting objects here. I will say instead that if you search for toilet paper origami on any internet search engine, the images that are online are impressive.

Number 40: China makes most of it

Toilet paper was invented in China. Therefore, it only makes sense that they would manufacture more of the stuff than any other nation. They have also seen a considerable amount of growth.

In 2018, for example, manufacturers in China produced a total of 104.35 million metric tons of paper in form or another. That figure includes not only paper intended for sanitary uses but also writing paper, newsprint, and so on. This means that they made 29.4% of all the paper in the world last year.

Looking specifically at facial and toilet tissue, China manufactured 9.7 million metric tons of it in 2018 or 30.7% of global production. The United States, by the way, came in second place 2018, having produced 6.95 million metric tons or 22% of the total global production for toilet paper. (Food and Agriculture Organization of the United Nations)

It seems mildly appropriate to me that the people who invented toilet paper more than a thousand years ago would still be making more of it than anyone else.

Number 41: Blasters

Once upon a time, kids used toilet paper and saliva to make spit balls that they would pelt someone with. It wasn't the proudest moment in human development, but it happened.

One of the things that I discovered while researching this project, is a little gizmo called the Toilet Paper Blaster. If you've never seen one of these things, allow me to describe it.

The Toilet Paper Blaster resembles somewhat a plastic rifle that any kid might play with. This one, however, has two important additions to it: a water bottle on top of it and a spool that holds a toilet paper roll on the side of it.

It automates the combining of toilet paper and water to make a projectile. It's also fires that toilet paper projectile at a target. As a bonus, since it uses water rather than saliva, clean up afterwards is much easier than with the old-fashioned spit ball.

I want to say that I have absolutely connection to manufacturers, distributors, or sellers of the Toilet Paper Blaster. No one paid me to include this toy in my book. It was just one of the many things that I came across while doing my research and one of the 50 that I thought were interesting enough to include.

Photos and video of the Toilet Paper Blaster are available on Amazon. I'm confident you will be able to see them elsewhere but that's where I saw it.

I invite you to check it out.

Number 42: Toilet-related injuries

While researching toilet paper, I stumbled across a number of claims of people being injured by a toilet, while on a toilet, or in some other manner that is related to toilets. Most of these turned out to be urban legends. Others have very little documentation to back them up so they may or may not be true.

As a related note, when I was researching this topic, the small bit of hard data that I could find was in a report from 2011 by the Centers for Disease Control & Prevention. In their introduction, the authors made a point of discussing is how challenging it is to get reliable data on toilet-related injuries. (Stevens, PhD and Hass)

The one thing that is clear from the data is that a person is more likely to suffer an injury in their bathroom than anywhere else in their home. It's a relatively small space that frequently has wet floors with lots of hard objects (tubs, sinks, etc.) to bang ones head on in the event of a fall.

With all of that said, there are a couple of anecdotes that I confirm as being accurate and worth of repeating. My favorite one, though, is the story about the World War II submarine that was sunk because of its toilet.

The German submarine U-1206 was on patrol in the North Sea, not far from Scotland, on April 14, 1945. It was less than two months from the end of the war in Europe. The toilet aboard backed up that day – possibly caused by a clog of toilet paper, though that part has never been confirmed.

Water from that toilet overflowed, eventually dripping onto the batteries located in an adjacent compartment. When the water made contact with those batteries, it formed chlorine gas. As the chlorine gas began to fill the submarine, her captain had no choice but head to the surface immediately in order to vent the toxic gas away.

Once on the surface, it was soon noticed by the Allies who attacked at once. With their submarine badly damaged, the German sailors had no choice but to scuttle their boat.

Thus, their U boat was ultimately done in by toilet. One German sailor never made it out of the submarine. Two more drowned after abandoning their boat. The remainder became prisoners of war. (Niesle)

Number 43: Alternatives for preppers

For those who believe in being prepared for a worst-case scenario, toilet paper is one the challenges in their preparations. If the end of the world as we now it arrives tomorrow, those who survive will still need to go to the bathroom and running out to the store for a few rolls isn't an option.

One of the more common options, is to buy toilet paper in bulk and store it. After all, it's not like the stuff has an expiration date. As long as it stays dry, it can be stored for years.

The downside is that it does take up storage space. One of the alternatives for those who don't have that much space or want to use their storage space for things other than toilet paper, there are also compressed coin tissues. These are small tablets – not much larger than a quarter – of a compressed tissue. When water is added, they will expand quickly to a usable sheet.

If neither of those options work, survivalists have all of the options that humans used for millennia prior to the invention of toilet paper. This includes pinecones, leaves, moss, stones, and so on.

Number 44: Killed by toilet paper

Toilet paper is nothing if not ubiquitous. Before I started researching for this project, however, I couldn't imagine that it could actually be used to cause someone's death.

In reality, there have been at least two instances where people used toilet paper as a way method of committing suicide. It was also used as a murder weapon in at least one documented instance.

Late one evening in 2011, a 91-year old woman was found dead in the bedroom of her nursing home in Tours, France. Various types of paper were found around her body and toilet paper was protruding from her mouth. An autopsy later confirmed that someone had stuffed a large amount of toilet paper down her throat causing her to suffocate.

A police investigation later determined that she was murdered by one of her fellow residents at the home. No motive for the crime was ever determined. (Saint-Martin, MD, Lefranq, MD and Sauvageau, MD, M.Sc.)

There are also two confirmed cases in which a mentally person committed suicide by shoving large amounts of toilet paper down their own throats resulting in them chocking to death. The first known instance was in 2006 when a 56-year old schizophrenic man ended his life. This was followed a year later by a second suicide by a 30-year old man killed himself while in the psychiatric ward of a hospital. (Saint-Martin, Bouyssy and O'Byrne) and (Sauvageau and Yesovitch)

Number 45: Weird nicknames

While researching for this book, I came across a plethora of nicknames for toilet paper. Below is my list of the ones that I saw, in no particular order.

- Moon squares
- Certificates of deposit
- Landing pad
- Ghetto Kleenex
- Tee-pee
- Mountain money
- Fireman's blanket
- Smudge rubs
- Crap-kerchief
- Butt wipes
- Bathroom tissue (technically, not a nickname but still...)
- Potty paper

A couple on this list made me groan. One or two made me laugh. In the end, though, I will continue to call the stuff toilet paper only.

Number 46: Government spending

One of the questions that fascinated me during my research for this project is the idea of government spending on something ordinary like toilet paper. We have lots of information about what consumers spend their money on – the brands we buy, where we buy them, when we are most likely to go shopping, and so on – is track by marketers

When government's buy something, however, the data is more hit and miss. Sometimes, there is a lot of data out there. Other times, it's spotty at best.

As someone who has spent entire days searching through government databases, I can attest that purchasing toilet paper is one of those areas of where information is surprising limited. One can readily discover the results of an experiment that the Agricultural Research Service did that used toilet paper to measure foraging done by termites. How much the U.S. Department of Agriculture spent for the toilet paper in that study, however, isn't readily available.

As I searched through news articles, I could find dozens of examples where one person used toilet paper as an example of the convoluted world of government purchasing; how the federal and state governments are filled with cumbersome rules that aren't as easy as going to your local store to pick up a few rolls. None of those articles, however, talk about how much is actually spent on it.

Occasionally, one will find a few clues here and there. For example, I found a request for bids from the U.S. Bureau of Prisons when they were looking to buy 35,000 rolls of the stuff. There's no data readily available as to what the winning bid was or what the aggregate totals were for spending on it in a given year.

There are also numerous examples online where one reporter or another spent weeks sifting through mountains of data to find instances of ridiculous purchases by the military and others. However, none of them are about toilet paper.

The one exception to that was when *Mother Jones* reported that the military spent an average of $2 million per year on toilet paper to support its 1.3 million active duty personnel from 2000 – 2010. There's nothing out there, however, for spending after 2010 or what the rest of the government spending was like. (Gilson)

After all of this time, I conclude that there are three distinct explanations for all of this.

- Government spending on toilet paper is, for the most part, scandal-free and thus news organizations don't cover it.
- It's so mundane that no one thinks about it except for when they are trying to think of an example of something that is really mundane.
- Toilet paper spending is ultra-secret because it's somehow tied to a conspiracy involving UFOs and Lizard People.

I will leave it to decide which one of those options is the most likely.

Number 47: Toilet paper tornado

I don't know who came up with the idea first. I spent a couple of hours looking into that questions but could never find the answer. All that I know is someone somewhere got the idea to attach a length of toilet paper to a fan and then to turn said fan on. The result of doing this is a spinning vortex of toilet paper.

There are several videos of this online. I encourage my readers to type the words "toilet paper tornado" into their internet search engine of choice and then say goodbye to the rest of their day.

Also, if anyone ever has any interest in trying such a thing at home then:

1. On the advice of my attorneys, I hereby expressly disavow any liability from damages and/or injuries that may result from anyone trying this as well as any associated cleanup costs. There almost certainly will be cleanup costs for anyone who tries this. Additional damages are a distinct possibility.
2. I'm told that cheap, lightweight toilet paper works best for this.

Personally, I will stick to watching the videos of this that are available online.

Number 48: You can't always flush it

It has always seemed to me that when one is done with toilet paper, the natural thing is to drop it into the toilet and flush it away with your bodily waste. I discovered, however, that there are several countries in the world where doing so can cause their toilets to become blocked up very quickly. As a result, one is supposed to dispose of the used toilet paper in a bin kept near the toilet.

This isn't something that is unique to third-world countries, which is the first thing that I thought when I encountered this phenomena. Below is a list in alphabetical order where people are discouraged from flushing toilet paper.

- Belarus
- Bolivia
- Bosnia Herzegovina
- Bulgaria
- Cyprus
- Egypt
- Greece
- Macedonia
- Moldova
- Montenegro
- Turkey
- Ukraine

There may well be other countries around the world where one can't flush toilet paper. There are simply the ones that I found during my research. (Coffey), (Romano), and (Cox)

Number 49: Start ups

These days it seems that there is a startup that is seeking to disrupt every industry in existence. A small (at first) firm who offers a seemingly crazy way of doing things.

Brick and mortar stores were disrupted by Amazon and eBay.

Taxi cabs were disrupted by Lyft and Uber.

Hotels and motels were disrupted by Airbnb and HomeAway.

Travel agencies were disrupted by Expedia, Kayak, and Travelocity.

The list goes on and on.

It was only a matter of time until someone found a way to disrupt the toilet paper industry. Several startups have emerged in recent years that are looking to change how we go to the bathroom. Companies like Better Planet, Cheeky Panda, Number 2, Tushy, and Who Gives A Crap.

Better Planet, for example, gives away environmentally-friendly toilet paper for free and plants a tree every time they ship an order. They even have a goal of planting 100 million trees The Florida-based company started as a joke but then raised $1 million in seed funding. (Christopher)

Who Gives A Crap makes all of their toilet paper from bamboo rather than freshly cut down trees. According to their website, they also donate 50% of their profits to help build toilets in the developing world.

Cheeky Panda makes not only toilet paper but diapers, paper towels, and biodegradable wipes, according to their website. They also produce everything using bamboo like a panda (cheeky or otherwise would do) and ensure that everything is free of plastics.

Number 2 advertises on its website that its toilet paper has 95% less Butt Crumble™. This is a rather unique way of describing the fact that their product is stronger and doesn't fall apart while being used.

Finally, Tushy does away with the whole concept of toilet paper. Their product converts any toilet into a bidet.

Again, I want to emphasize that I have absolutely no commercial or personal relationship with anyone from any of these companies. These are simply things that I found while researching for this project that I thought were worth repeating.

Number 50: This cartoon

I came across this cartoon while researching for this book at the Library of Congress. It was originally made in England in 1754. The simple fact that toilet paper was used in a cartoon 265 years ago astonishes me almost as much as the wedding dresses made from toilet paper did.

Etching shows four persons seated at a table, a waiter drawing a cork from a jug, and William Hogarth, "A", standing, saying, "Give me some waste paper Jack." Two artists at the table offer him their work to be used as toilet paper. Below is a list "Persons of Worth, Encouragers of Art" (left) and a poem addressed to Hogarth (right). (A Club of Artist's)

Conclusion

If you had told me a few months ago that I would one day write a book on toilet paper, there is simply no way that I would have believed you. This project started as an idea that came to me at 3 o'clock in the morning. After all of this time researching, writing, and edition, my finish product is now in your hands.

My only wish at that when next you are using the facilities; you pause for an instant to remember the roughly 1,500 years of history that went into that roll of paper near you. For men like John Gayetty and the Scott Brothers, it was an idea that consumed much of their lives.

I can only presume that it also consumed much of the life of an ancient inventor in China as well. His or her name has long since been lost to antiquity but that roll of paper was likely a big part of his or her life regardless.

All of this is a reminder that everything in our lives has a story behind it. I hope you will get a chance to hear all of those stories.

If you would be so kind, I would also ask that you take a moment to leave a review of this book on Amazon or whatever other service it was where you found it. Whether you tell the world how much you hated my writing or how much you enjoyed, the act of reviewing a book does a lot to help others discover my work.

Thank you.

Works Cited

"A Club of Artist's." England: Retrieved from the Library of Congress, 1754.

American Forest and Paper Association. "Facts About the Use of Bleaching Agents in Tissue and Paper Towel Manufacturing." n.d. *American Forest and Paper Association.* 31 October 2019.

Bird, Mike. "An economist just explained Venezuela's chronic shortage of toilet paper." 10 November 2010. *Business Insider.* 5 November 2018.

Boone, John. "Beyoncé's Alleged Tour Demands (Red Toilet Paper! No Junk Food!) Ranked in Terms of Divaness." 1 May 2013. *E! Online.* 30 October 2019.

Christopher, Eric. "It Started As a Joke and Turned Into a Startup That Raised $1 Million in Funding." 12 September 2018. *Entrepreneur.* 1 November 2019.

Clean It Supply. "Do Plies Really Make a Difference in Toilet Paper Quality?" 23 August 2010. *Clean It Supply.* 2019 October 2019.

Coffey, Helen. "MAPPED: You CAN'T flush toilet paper down the loo in THESE 10 European countries." 19 March 2017. *The Sunday Express.* 3 November 2019.

Cox, Amanda. "Don't flush the toilet paper! – Access to basic services in Bolivia." 12 April 2017. *Amanda Around The World.* 1 November 2019.

DW. "German non-profit flushes away right-wing hate." 15 September 2017. *DW.* 29 October 2019.

Earley, Catherine Thérèse. "The Greatest Missed Luxury." Fakk 2010. *Pennsylvania Center for the Book.* 31 October 2019.

Fischburg, Kenn. "What is Toilet Paper Made of?" 26 August 2016. *Supply Time.* 30 October 2019.

Food and Agriculture Organization of the United Nations. *Pulp and paper capacities survey*. Series. Rome: FAO, 2019.

Gilson, Dave. "Let's Roll: Unraveling the Pentagon's Toilet Paper Budget." 19 December 2013. *Mother Jones.* 2 November 2019.

Hart, Peter W. and Alan Rudie. "Hydrogen peroxide : an environmentally friendly but dangerous bleaching chemical." *Proceedings of TAPPI engineering, pulping and environmental conference* 21-23 October 2007. Online.

Hernández, Javier C. "China's High-Tech Tool to Fight Toilet Paper Bandits." 20 March 2017. *The New York Times.* 31 October 2019.

History of Toilet Paper. *Toilet Paper Fun Facts*. 2019. 30 October 2019.

James, Geoffrey. "The Correct Way to Hang Toilet Paper, According to Science." 8 August 2014. *Inc.* 30 October 2019.

Khetani-Shah, Sanya and Jillian Deutsch. "Brexit timeline: From referendum to EU exit." 25 August 2017. *Politico Pro.* 3 November 2019.

Lazarus, David. "Ask Laz: Toilet paper: Bigger cardboard rolls, smaller sheets, same price." 21 January 2015. *Los Angeles Times.* 30 October 2019.

Lustig, M., et al. "Beware of the toilet: The risk for a deep tissue injury during toilet sitting." *Journal of Tissue Viability* (2018): 23-31.

Mansfield University of Pennsylvania. *Mansfield History - Timeline*. 2019. https://www.mansfield.edu/mansfield-history/timeline/1800s.cfm. 28 October 2019.

Molina, Brett. "How do astronauts poop in space? NASA astronaut Peggy Whitson explains." 30 May 2018. *USA Today*. 30 October 2019.

National Institute for Occupational Safety & Health. "Workplace Safety & Health Concerns: Chlorine." 26 June 2018. *Centers for Disease Control & Prevention*. 31 October 2019.

Needham, Joseph. *Science and Civilization in China: Volume 5, Chemistry and Chemical Technology, Part 1, Paper and Printing*. Taipei: Caves Books, Ltd, 1986. 30 October 2019.

Ng, Serena. "Toilet-Tissue 'Desheeting' Shrinks Rolls, Plumps Margins." 24 July 2013. *Wall Street Journal*. 30 October 2019.

Niesle, Axel. *German U-Boat Losses During World War II*. Bethesda: United States Naval Institute, 1998.

QSR. "Bagasse Paper Products Now Available from Sugar Cane Paper Company." 10 September 2008. *QSR*. 30 October 2019.

Romano, Andrea. "Bathroom Etiquette Around The World So You Can Know Before You Go." 7 July 2017. *Travel & Leisure*. 26 October 2019.

Saint-Martin, MD, Pauline, Thierry Lefranq, MD and Anny
        Sauvageau, MD, M.Sc. "Homicidal smothering on toilet
        paper: A case report." *Journal of Forensic and Legal
        Medicine* (2012): 234-5.

Saint-Martin, P., M. Bouyssy and P O'Byrne. "An unusual case of
        suicidal asphyxia by smothering." *Journal of Forensic
        and Legal Medicine* (2007): 39-41.

Sauvageau, A. and R. Yesovitch. "Choking on toilet paper: an
        unusual case of suicide and a review of the literature on
        suicide by smothering, strangulation, and choking."
        American Journal of Forensic Medicine and Pathology
        (2006): 173-4.

Scott Paper Company. *A Long History of Firsts*. 2019.
        https://www.scottbrand.com/en-us/about-us/ourstory.
        29 October 2019.

Shaerf, Nick. "Johnny Carson and the Toilet Paper Scare of '73."
        19 July 2019. *Paley Center for Media.* 1 November 2019.

Shahbandeh, M. "Sales of the leading 10 toilet tissue brands of
        the U.S. 2017." 12 July 2018. *Statista.* 29 October 2019.

Slawski, Bill. "Google's most popular and least popular top level
        domains." 13 January 2006. *SEO by the sea.* 1 November
        2019.

Spooky. "Fit for a Royal Behind – Hanebisho, the World's Most
        Expensive Toilet Paper That Costs $17 a Roll." 28 August
        2013. *Oddity Central.* 30 October 2019.

Statista. "Amount of toilet paper used within 30 days in the U.S.
        2019." 31 August 2019. *Statista.* 31 October 2019.

Stevens, PhD, Judy A. and Elizabeth N. Hass. "Nonfatal
        Bathroom Injuries Among Persons Aged ≥15 Years." 10

June 2011. *Morbidity & Mortality Weekly Report.* 30 October 2019.

Taylor, Ian. "Toilet paper and spread of infection." *British Medical Journal* (1978): 1024.

The Dredge. "Chrissy Teigen has revealed how celebrities buy toilet paper... ." 19 July 2016. *The Dredge.* 31 October 2019.

The Telegraph. "Golden hoovers and luxury lavs: The 10 most expensive household items." *The Telegraph* 11 May 2016.

Travel China Guide. "Temple of Heaven." 9 October 2019. *Travel China Guide.* 31 October 2019.

Wolf, Buck. "Great Moments in Toilet Paper History." 23 April 2002. *ABC News.* 2 November 2019.

Woodruff, Mandi. "The True Cost Of Our $30 Billion Obsession With Toilet Paper." 17 May 2013. *Business Insider.* 31 October 2019.

World Population Review. "Countries ranked by GDP 2019." 2019. *World Population Review.* 31 October 2019.

Worldometer. *World Population.* October 2019. 30 October 2019.